SAINTS

in Medieval Manuscripts

SAINTS
in Medieval Manuscripts

GREG BUZWELL

THE BRITISH LIBRARY

INTRODUCTION:
SAINTS IN THE MEDIEVAL WORLD

Devotion to the saints played a crucial role in the religious life of the Middle Ages. Kings and queens, merchants and craftsmen, beggars and thieves – all were alike in drawing inspiration, reassurance and solace from the lives of holy martyrs and pious confessors. Saints were much loved because they held a unique position in the hierarchy of Heaven; they had the power to intercede directly with God on behalf of the living. On a personal level, people prayed for saints to intervene as they faced the inevitable perils of the human condition: the sufferings of childbirth, the hardships of a lengthy journey or the ever-present threat of plague. Similarly, on a grand historic scale, monarchs asked the saints to aid their political and military ambitions: King Henry V of England invoked St George in order to rally his dispirited and outnumbered troops as they prepared to face a vast French force near the town of Agincourt. Some years later, in the same conflict, the French fought back with spectacular success as they rallied around a young girl, Joan of Arc, who had been divinely inspired by the voices of St Michael, St Catherine of Alexandria and St Margaret of Antioch. Whether in the making of history or in the everyday moments of unrecorded lives, the saints were always in the minds of the people.

Today many of the legends and tales told about the saints have become so deeply embedded in the fabric of society that they have, in effect, crossed the boundary between religious hagiography (writing of the lives of the saints) and folklore, thus entering a world of common cultural history. St George (1) charging towards a dragon in order to rescue a fair maiden; St Patrick casting out all the snakes from Ireland; St Antony suffering visions, torments and temptations: all are well known, even to those of a non-Catholic persuasion. And yet for each easily recognisable saint there are dozens who are genuinely obscure: St Juthwara, for instance, an English West Country saint whose martyrdom reputedly came about as a bizarre consequence of a remedy for chest pains involving a pair of cheeses; and St Wilgefortis (2) the bearded female saint, daughter of a pagan Portuguese king, who could be invoked by wives wishing to rid themselves of unwanted husbands.

1. *St George and the dragon, c. 1474. Additional MS 15702, f.239v.*

2. St Wilgefortis who could be asked to remove an unwanted husband, late fifteenth to early sixteenth century. *Additional MS 19416, f.145v.*

Familiar though many saints may be, some elements of their history are not immediately obvious. How does someone become a saint? Who were the first saints? Why was devotion to the saints so passionate? Why did certain individuals, professions, towns and countries adopt particular saints as their patrons? Why are certain saints so routinely depicted in standard poses and with such distinctive objects or creatures – St Lucy, for example, carrying a tray on which lies a pair of eyes, or St Margaret of Antioch (3) emerging unharmed from the inside of a dragon? Why were a saint's relics so important and why were pilgrimages to their shrines so popular? Finally, why were images of saints attacked with such ferocity when medieval ecclesiastical practices and beliefs were challenged throughout much of Europe during the Reformation in the sixteenth century?

With such a vast array of saints to choose from, it would be impossible in a book of this size to go into detail about the lives, legends, depictions and relevance of any but a very small number. The selection made here is personal and is centred on those saints whose cults are based in the Latin West. Some, St Sebastian and St George for example, are well known, but many less familiar saints are also included. All are illustrated with examples primarily taken from The British Library's collection of medieval Western manuscripts, and the particular nature of these manuscripts and their importance in medieval religious life is also discussed.

3. *St Margaret emerges unharmed from the stomach of a dragon, fifteenth century. Harley MS 2974, f.165v.*

MARTYRS

In the Judaeo-Christian tradition a saint is a person of holy character, venerated as an example of both religious and personal excellence and for having lived a life in 'imitation of Christ'. The veneration of saints in the Christian church has a history stretching back to the second century. Beginning with the martyrs and then evolving to include virgin martyrs, theologians, visionaries, mystics, monastics and missionaries, the paths to sainthood have become more varied with time, and the process by which an individual comes to be regarded as a saint has changed considerably. In order to understand the ever-changing nature of sainthood, it is perhaps easiest to return to the very beginning and examine the case of the first saints (excluding the Virgin, John the Baptist and the apostles) – namely the martyrs.

The word martyr means 'witness'. In Christian terminology a martyr, or witness of Christ, is an individual who, despite never having seen at first hand the Divine Founder of the Church, is yet so firmly convinced of the truths of the Christian religion that he would rather face death than deny his beliefs. Christians were first the victims of persecution around AD 64 when the Emperor Nero, looking for a way in which to divert attention from his own unpopularity, singled them out as a particularly pernicious enemy of the Roman Empire. Many Christians were crucified or beheaded while others were thrown to the lions for the entertainment of the people. Reputedly many were burnt to death at night in order to provide lighting for the emperor's gardens. The persecutions continued on and off for almost two hundred and fifty years until,

4. *St Stephen, stoned to death, early fifteenth century. Additional MS 29433, f.202v.*

in AD 313, the Emperor Constantine established a lasting peace. Those who died for their beliefs were held in particularly high regard by their fellow Christians. It was commonly believed that a martyr who lost his life through love and belief in Christ would be assured a seat in Heaven and, thereby, would be able to exercise intercessory prayer on behalf of those who invoked him. The anniversary of a martyr's death (the *natalis*, or birthday in Heaven) was commemorated with a feast. Initially, only the local community commemorated the martyr's passing, but gradually the cult of various martyrs spread – often as a result of miracles said to have occurred in the vicinity of the burial place – and over the years an ever-growing section of the Christian world commemorated the martyr's death and the miracles performed in his name.

Among the martyrs most commonly depicted in medieval manuscripts are Saints Stephen, Sebastian and Laurence. Stephen (d. c. AD 35) (4) was the first official Christian martyr, the protomartyr, one of the seven deacons appointed by the apostles to help form the basis of the new church. He argued

that the Jews were refusing to recognise the Messiah and denying the Holy Spirit. Enraged by his accusations, the priests dragged him from the city and had him stoned to death.

The existence of St Stephen is a matter of historical fact, his martyrdom having been witnessed by Saul (better known to the world as St Paul following his conversion on the road to Damascus). The story of St Sebastian is cloudier although still grounded in fact. St Sebastian (5) was a Roman soldier martyred during the reign of the Emperor Diocletian c. AD 300 and buried in a cemetery near the Appian Way, close to

5. *Martyrdom of St Sebastian, late fourteenth century. Additional MS 23145, f.34v.*

6. Martyrdom of St Laurence, latter half of fifteenth century. Egerton MS 2019, f.209.

the basilica just outside the walls of Rome, which bears his name. Denounced and condemned for his Christian beliefs, the emperor ordered Sebastian be executed by a hail of arrows. Once the order had been carried out Sebastian was left for dead but, miraculously, he recovered and returned to confront the emperor who ordered he be clubbed to death. In art, St Sebastian is often shown tied to a tree or post, standing before archers, and with his body pierced by numerous arrows, an image which conveys the full depth of his suffering and the callous barbarity of his persecutors. During the mid-fourteenth century, St Sebastian — sometimes referred to by the less than pious epithet 'The Holy Pincushion' — was frequently invoked by those stricken with plague because of his ability to recover from the disfiguring wounds of the arrows, wounds which mirrored the buboes caused by the Black Death.

The suffering of St Laurence is arguably even more gruesome. According to legend Laurence (6), a deacon of Rome, was roasted to death on a gridiron. His existence and his martyrdom are confirmed by very ancient sources, but, at the time of his martyrdom, beheading with a sword was the usual form of execution and there appears to be no historical evidence to substantiate the common story of his death. Fact and myth intertwine to make the lesson of the saint's martyrdom all the more persuasive. Historical fact may have been pushed to one side in this instance, but the worlds of art and pious imagination have gained immeasurably from the legend as it stands and Laurence has become a much-loved saint throughout the Western world.

VIRGIN MARTYRS

The female counterparts of the martyrs were the 'virgin martyrs'. In the early Christian church celibacy was synonymous with holiness, so virginity, as proof of female sexual abstinence, was held in high regard. Given such dire warnings as that in the book of Ecclesiasticus 'From woman came the beginning of sin, and by her we all die', women who drew away from earthly desires and devoted their lives to God were prominently positioned in the holy hierarchy. Many of the best-known saints fall into the category of virgin martyrs, and their legends – which tend towards the colourful and the imaginative in any case – usually contain an extra element which is missing from the more factual accounts of their male counterparts. Not only do they face death for refusing to renounce

7. St Catherine of Alexandria with the attributes of her learning and martyrdom, fifteenth century. Yates Thompson 3, f.281v.

their religious beliefs, but they must also resist nefarious sexual advances. They are routinely tempted by offers of marriage from emperors and lords; incredible wealth can be theirs if they renounce their Christian beliefs and worship the pagan gods of the Roman State religion. For their refusal to comply they are tortured and executed.

One such virgin martyr, St Catherine of Alexandria, proved to be so popular with medieval artists that after the Blessed Virgin Mary herself she has a strong claim to being the most frequently portrayed saint in the history of art. Her usual attributes, as depicted in this beautiful and serene illustration (7) from a fifteenth-century French Book of Hours which once belonged to Jean Dunois, companion in arms of Joan of Arc, are the spiked wheel and the sword, both of which form part of her suffering and eventual martyrdom. In this image she is also shown reading, an indication of her piety and knowledge of the scriptures. Her origin is obscure – there is no ancient cult for St Catherine, no mention in early martyrologies and no early works of art. She was supposedly martyred in the fourth century but it was not until the ninth century that her ascendancy and popularity began – centred on Mount Sinai, to which angels reputedly carried her body after her execution. Veneration for St Catherine soon became established in the East, but it was only with the return of the first crusaders from the Holy Land in the late eleventh and early twelfth centuries that her cult took hold in the West. According to legend, Catherine was born in Alexandria to a noble family and converted to Christianity, after seeing a vision of Mary and the Christ child. Her refusal to worship the idols of the Roman State religion attracted the attention of the emperor Maxentius. The emperor's determination to prove her incorrect in her belief led to the much-told tale of the fifty pagan philosophers brought in especially to dispute with the young woman. Catherine's arguments were so successful that all fifty converted to Christianity, whereupon the emperor promptly ordered they be burnt to death. In some accounts the emperor proposes marriage to Catherine, but she refuses on the grounds that she is already 'the bride of Christ' (in art she is often depicted receiving a wedding ring from the infant Jesus). Maxentius eventually issued orders demanding she be tied and broken on an elaborate spiked wheel, but no sooner had the wheel been brought into place than it exploded, killing its operators (the Catherine Wheel firework takes its name from this legend). Finally, the emperor opted for a more straightforward

8. Martyrdom and burial of St Catherine of Alexandria, fifteenth century. Additional MS 11865, f.90.

method of getting rid of her and had her beheaded. In this illustration (8), taken from another fifteenth-century French Book of Hours, the artist has depicted the final scenes of St Catherine's life. The wheel is destroyed by divine intervention. Maxentius then has her beheaded, after which angels (perhaps a misinterpretation in the written sources for 'monks' who were often described as living an 'angelic' life) carry her body to Mount Sinai. In the legend, milk rather than blood flowed from the saint's neck after her death but here, perhaps revelling in the opportunity to depict something truly horrific, the artist has chosen to portray a stream of crimson blood issuing from the severed arteries. The whole story is wildly improbable and the brief account given above is only one variation on a number of similar tales told about her life. Indeed, there is almost nothing in the way of historical evidence to back up any of the many and varied elements of her legend. The Holy See went so far as to suppress the cult of St Catherine, along with those of many other virgin martyrs, in 1969. As with the tale of St Laurence and the gridiron, however, the general gain to the world of art that has arisen from her colourful legend is incalculable. In England alone more than fifty murals were painted depicting scenes from her legend, while her life, as well as being depicted in manuscripts (9) is also shown in many stained glass windows, including a notable series at York Minster.

Early written hagiography tended to follow a set pattern: confrontation with figures of state authority, trial, sentencing, torture, execution, burial and posthumous miracles. The legend of St Barbara, imprisoned in a tower by her father Dioscorus, is a typical example. His intention was to keep her hidden from the eyes of potential male suitors, but while thus walled away from the world she converted to Christianity, asking the architects of the tower to add a third window in honour of the Holy Trinity, and chose to live as a hermit. Dioscorus was furious to hear of her religious conversion and dragged her to the authorities. Barbara was sentenced to death by beheading for her religious beliefs and her father himself struck the fatal blow, following which he was promptly reduced to a heap of smouldering ashes by a bolt of fire from the sky. In an illumination from the Breviary of Queen Isabella of Spain, St Barbara (10) is shown sitting in a walled garden (a symbol of virginity) while reading a book (symbolising her learning). Beside her is the tower, the most famous element of her legend and the attribute most frequently depicted in her portrayal, while in the background, in the world outside the enclosed garden, scenes

9. *St Catherine of Alexandria trampling on a tyrant*, c. 1480. *Additional MS 54782, f.68v.*

10. *St Barbara with her tower, late fifteenth century. Additional MS 18851, f.297.*

from her life and martyrdom are played out. As a consequence of her father's celestial incineration, St Barbara was frequently invoked against lightning strikes and sudden death. By analogy, as the use of cannons became commonplace towards the very end of the Hundred Years War, she became the patron saint of gunners and artillerymen.

To see just how bizarre some legends about the virgin martyrs can be, one has only to consider the legend of St Juthwara as recorded in the *Nova Legenda Angliae*, a fifteenth-century anthology of the lives of English saints edited by John Capgrave, an Augustinian friar, historian and theologian. Much given to fasting and prayer, pious and devout Juthwara (11), a young girl from the English West Country, suffered from pains in her chest after her father's death – perhaps brought on by a surfeit of grief. Her stepmother, scheming and evil in true fairytale fashion, recommended she apply soft cheeses to her breasts in order to relieve the pain. Later Juthwara's stepmother told her own son, Bana, that the supposedly virginal Juthwara was pregnant. Bana confronted the frightened girl and, discovering that her tunic was moist (but not, curiously discovering any evidence of the cheeses) he struck off her head. Juthwara then carried her severed head back to the church – a sure sign of her innocence and virginity. Bana, faced with this disturbing and miraculous sight, not surprisingly repented and became a monk. As a legend it has a certain fairytale charm and a slightly sinister beauty, but as a pious legend it is little more than a stream of impossibilities.

11. *St Juthwara, with her severed head, 1399–1407. Additional MS 74236, p.489.*

Another curious tale concerns the virgin martyr, St Ursula (12), tortured by the Huns in the fourth century. She is often portrayed with an improbably large number of virginal companions – usually said to be 11,000, probably on account of an earlier misreading of an abbreviated text. The legend itself tells how Ursula, daughter of a British king, negotiated a three-year delay before her intended marriage to a pagan prince because she wished to remain a virgin. She passed the three years on a ship, cruising with ten companions each of whom occupied a ship of their own containing one thousand followers. Strong winds blew them to the Rhine where, because of their Christianity, they were martyred. The charming image shown here is typical in showing St Ursula with her multitude of companions.

In contrast to the virgin martyrs, St Mary Magdalene, one of the most popular female saints, reached sainthood by a highly circuitous route. Viewed from the totally male-centred perspective of the Middle Ages, the Blessed Virgin Mary and St Mary Magdalene represented the two opposing faces of womankind. Human frailty is rare

12. *St Ursula and the 11,000 virgins, late fifteenth century. Additional MS 18851, f.474v.*

in the fellowship of the saints. On the surface Mary Magdalene, with her scandalous past (cobbled together from various unconnected passages from the Bible, which did not always relate to the same woman), made her a questionable role model for women during the Middle Ages. Her later history however – the loving, forgiven sinner, privileged to be the first to see the risen Christ – makes her the supreme Christian penitent. Christianity in the medieval world tended to see women in purely sexual terms. Most female saints such as St Catherine and St Barbara were characterised by their virginity. Mary Magdalene was characterised by her redemption following a sinful life. Her penitence and Christ's forgiveness of her sins made her a much-loved saint for people all too aware of their own failings.

13. *St Mary Magdalene, with ointment jar, c. 1450. Harley MS 2915, f.152v.*

14. *St Mary Magdalene taken up to Heaven, fifteenth century. Yates Thompson 3, f.280.*

Mary Magdalene (13) is usually portrayed holding the pot containing the ointment with which she anointed the feet of Christ. The other striking aspect of her appearance is her long hair which, during the latter years of her life, grew to such a length it covered her entire body. In legend she lived out her final years in France and was borne up to Heaven seven times each day (14). As the patron saint of repentant sinners, Mary Magdalene was extremely popular in the Middle Ages. In England alone over 150 churches – not to mention colleges at both Oxford and Cambridge – were dedicated to her.

CONFESSOR SAINTS

The routes by which an individual can arrive at sainthood are many and varied. From AD 313 onwards, after the cessation of the persecution of Christians, teachers such as St Basil and St John Chrysostom proposed the idea that ordinary Christian life, when lived consistently in a spirit of loving self-offering to God, can in itself be regarded as a kind of martyrdom. By the close of the fourth century, the honours bestowed upon the martyrs of old were being extended to ascetics in the wilderness, who were seen as in some sense inflicting martyrdom on themselves in order to prove their love of God, and to outstanding bishops and teachers. Those honoured as saints without having suffered martyrdom are referred to as confessors – the term implying that by confessing the Christian faith in their lives they bear witness to Christ with as much passion as a martyr does by his or her death.

Eusebius Hieronymous, better known to the world as St Jerome (c. AD 341–420), is a good example of a confessor saint. Jerome spent much of his life in solitude in imitation of the desert fathers, denying himself the worldly trappings of success which his excellent eductation could have brought him, and is best known for his translation of the Bible from Hebrew into Latin. In art, as in this depiction (15), he is often anachronistically shown wrapped in a cardinal's cloak (cardinals were not created until many centuries after Jerome's death) and is often accompanied by a lion, a reference to the lion he healed and tamed after it had terrified the monks of a local monastery. He is also frequently shown holding a stone with which he repeatedly beat his breast. A difficult man with a fiery temper and something of a gift for inspiring resentment and jealousy, it was said of him by one Renaissance pope that he did well to beat his breast with a stone as there was little else about him which justified the term 'saint'.

Later came monastics such as Benedict (c. AD 480–550) and Bernard of Clairvaux (c. 1090–1153), and the founders of religious orders such as Dominic Guzman (c. 1170–1221) – who founded the Dominicans – and Francis of Assisi (1181–1226), founder of the Franciscan Order. The life of St Francis is extremely well documented. He was born in Assisi, the son of a wealthy draper, and led a relatively carefree life until he was taken prisoner in a minor conflict between Assisi

15. St Jerome in the wilderness, 1492–1503. Yates Thompson 29, f. 127v.

and Perugia. A year later, a chastened and more reflective man, he returned to Assisi and while praying in the derelict church of San Damiano he heard a voice telling him to repair the church. This he did, c. 1208, selling some of his father's cloth in order to do so – an action which inevitably caused a certain amount of tension between the two. Francis later became an itinerant preacher, initially attracting seven disciples who became, effectively, the foundation of the Franciscan Order. Many of the most famous moments in his life occurred in his final few years when he wrote the *Canticle of Brother Sun*, invented the Christmas crib and received the stigmata. Exhausted by his religious fervour and hard work he died in 1226, aged forty-five. He was canonized in 1228 – probably the shortest interval between death and canonization in the entire history of sainthood. His relics were transferred to a huge new basilica and monastery dedicated to him in Assisi. Depictions of St Francis in art are numerous, perhaps the most common represen-tations being the moment in 1224 when he received the stigmata on Mount Verna (16) or of the nature-loving saint preaching to the birds.

16. *St Francis of Assisi receives the stigmata, fifteenth century. Yates Thompson 3, f.288.*

CANONIZATION

Gradually, the casual manner in which popular acclaim was enough for an individual to be regarded as a saint was changed and made more formal. Towards the latter years of the tenth century, the growing prestige of the papacy led Christian communities to seek ratification from the pope for the translation or reburial of relics from tombs to altars. Approval from the pope enhanced a saint's cult considerably and over time the decision to canonize or not to canonize – that is to admit an individual formally into the roster of saints – became entirely the preserve of the papacy, something that was formally inscribed in the laws of the Roman Church, in the first half of the thirteenth century, during the papacy of Gregory IX.

Canonization takes the form of a lengthy enquiry into the life, works, piety and character of the person on whose behalf the process has been instituted. The procedure resembles a legal trial with advocates, witnesses and even a prosecuting council, usually referred to as a 'devil's advocate', appointed to argue against the candidate purely so that a balanced picture can be obtained. Miracles performed by the nominated candidate during his or her life, or said to have occurred after their death in the vicinity of their tomb, are given particular consideration. The papacy also reserves the right to approve certain local cults observed only within one particular diocese. Such beatification (from the Latin for 'blessing') has become a necessary prerequisite for canonization, although the former does not automatically lead to the latter. Pictorially, by the second half of the fourteenth century, the depiction of both the beatified and the canonized had been standardized. The beatified are shown with rays of light around their heads while the canonized have their heads gilded with golden haloes. Papal commissions were appointed to investigate and pronounce upon the sanctity or otherwise of the individuals and cults investigated. However, even then, a certain amount of shady dealing took place. It has been argued that the canonization of the English king, Edward the Confessor – whose claim for sainthood was promoted by King Henry II – may have been approved by Pope Alexander III more in recognition of the support he received from Henry II against the anti-pope, Victor IV, and the German Emperor, Frederic Barbarossa, than because of Edward's own pious virtues.

THE ROLE OF SAINTS, RELICS AND PILGRIMAGE

So, why were saints so important and so beloved of the people of the Western world? In popular belief the hierarchy of Heaven (17) was ordered along similar lines to the hierarchy on Earth: God as King, Christ as Prince, Mary as Queen and the saints acting as courtiers. Seen as intercessors between God and mankind (18), saints were there to heal the breach between God and the fallen world. During the Middle Ages, the saints represented the human and compassionate face of the Kingdom of Heaven. Their eternal existence in the divine presence of God made them figures of extreme power and their aid was frequently invoked for all manner of purposes such as protection in battle (19), relief from pain or for blessing your chosen trade.

If the Blessed Virgin Mary was the person to whom one addressed a plea for eternal salvation, then it was to any one of the vast array of saints that more everyday appeals for help were directed. Today, this remains the most familiar function of the saints; no matter the nature or severity of the affliction or concern, at least one of their vast number can be invoked to intercede with God on one's behalf. In many instances it was the nature of the saint's martyrdom that determined the particular area in which they could be asked to intercede. For example, part of the torture and martyrdom of St Apollonia (20), an aged deaconess of Alexandria whose suffering took place in AD 249, involved her jaw being broken, in consequence of which she was invoked against toothache. In the majority of depictions, like the one shown here, St Apollonia is portrayed as a young girl having her teeth extracted by turbaned ruffians (the turban in Western medieval art is usually used to denote a follower of pagan beliefs) using pincers. To this very day the saint is commemorated by a dentists' quarterly journal called 'The Apollonian', published in Boston, Massachusetts. Similarly, St Lucy, whose eyes were reputedly gouged out during her martyrdom, was called upon by those suffering diseases of the eye. St Roch (21), who lived as a hermit and suffered from the plague, was frequently invoked by those living in towns and villages threatened by pestilence. In other instances, however, the reason a saint came to be regarded as a patron of a particular group of people or cause is less immediately obvious.

17. The hierarchy in Heaven: The Virgin and Child with attendant archangels and saints, fourteenth century. Arundel 83, f.131v.

18. Saints Benedict and Paul acting as mediators between the earthly and the heavenly, 1330–50.
Royal MS 6 E VI, f.16.

19. *Normans praying before the relics of St Valery, 1470–80. Royal MS 15 F IV, f.223.*

St Jude became the patron saint of lost causes because, initially, nobody ever invoked him for anything since his name so closely resembled that of Judas, the betrayer of Christ.

Individuals, towns, cities and countries put themselves under the patronage of particular saints. The Virgin was universally venerated, but from so many saints each Catholic chose one especially to honour: a patron saint. Thomas More, for example, Henry VIII's chancellor and a staunch defender of the Catholic faith during the early years of the Reformation, chose St Thomas the Apostle – 'Doubting Thomas', one of the few saints who displayed an all too human failing – as his patron. Privately honouring one saint in particular was perfectly permissible, but in general it was expected that the whole body of saints should be honoured by the faithful, something the Church promoted on the feast of All Saints.

The inhabitants of a particular area usually adopted as their chosen patron a saint who had once lived amongst them. The citizens of Paris adopted St Geneviève, holding her in specifically high regard and viewing her as a role model following her heroic actions in defending the city against marauding Huns and Franks during the

20. *Martyrdom of St Apollonia, latter half of fifteenth century. Egerton MS 2019, f.217.*

21. St Roch, pictured with the dog who brought him food during his time of suffering, early sixteenth century. Egerton MS 2125, f.209v.

fifth century. All through the Middle Ages her feretory (a shrine for a saint's relics) was routinely carried around the city by the inhabitants as they invoked her aid in times of plague or war. On a smaller scale, but with a similar show of devotion and affection, the people of the isolated community of Morebath, on the southern edge of Exmoor in Devon, adopted St Sidwell as their patron and saved diligently in order to commission and erect a statue of her in their village church – a statue sadly only completed just in time to be pulled down during the Reformation. Born in Exeter, and a distinctly shadowy figure, St Sidwell, or Sativola as she is sometimes known, was a Saxon virgin. She was a girl of great piety, murdered on the instructions of her stepmother who ordered the reapers in the field to decapitate her with their scythes. Devotion to a local saint such as St Sidwell was a powerful influence and the cause for a considerable amount of pride. Roger Keyes (d. 1477), canon of Exeter, saw to it that this obscure West Country saint was included in the stained glass and

wall paintings of both Eton College, Windsor and All Souls, Oxford while he was overseeing their construction. Professions, as we have already seen with dentists, also adopted saints. As legendary portraitist of the Virgin Mary, the apostle St Luke (22) became the patron saint of artists. Similarly St Catherine of Alexandria, because of the elaborate wheel on which the Emperor Maxentius intended to have her martyred, was adopted as the patron saint of wheelwrights, spinners and millers.

RELICS

A saint's relics – bones, primarily, but also the clothes the saint had worn and the instruments of his or her martyrdom – were believed to offer protection against ill health and misfortune. It was believed that on the day of judgement the bones would

be transformed into the living body of the saint and, consequently, they were of extreme value to the Church and were seen by the populace as having an almost magical property (23). Once the relics were moved, or 'translated', from a tomb to a church altar they could be divided and split into fragments, thus increasing the number of churches which could have relics of their own (24). Relics attracted pilgrims and pilgrims attracted trade, so the market in relics soon became of considerable interest for the Church as a whole. This importance placed on a saint's

23. *A bishop moving a saint's relics to a niche in an altar, fourteenth century. Lansdowne MS 451, f.236v.*

bodily remains, both spiritually and financially, has led to many macabre incidents. Legend has it that early in the eleventh century, a group of Umbrian peasants plotted to kill the hermit St Romuald in order to secure the possession of his precious bones.

24. *The procession of St Alban's relics, 1250–54. Cotton Nero D I, f.22.*

Hugh of Lincoln (c. 1140–1200), himself later canonized, was given the honour while visiting the Abbey at Fécamp in Normandy of viewing bones from the arm of Mary Magdalene. Unwrapping the bones from their protective cloth he then attempted, while making a play of kissing the holy relics, to bite off a small fragment, first delicately with his incisors and then rather more blatantly with his molars. In 1231, at the lying in state of St Elizabeth of Hungary, a crowd of worshippers cut or tore strips of the linen covering her face while others hacked locks from her hair and pulled out her fingernails. In 1392 King Charles VI of France, never renowned for his sound and rational behaviour, was seen to distribute ribs from his ancestor St Louis to his relatives during a solemn feast. Today, many find the display of uncorrupted corpses, such as that of Clare of Assisi (d. 1253), within glass coffins a little macabre.

PILGRIMAGE

The idea of pilgrimage, the belief that it is desirable – or even essential – to undertake a journey to a shrine in order to achieve renewed spiritual purity or to expiate a particularly grave sin, goes back far into antiquity. The concept of pilgrimage is familiar to many religions: Jews are obliged to journey to Jerusalem, Hindus journey to the Ganges and Muslims undertake journeys to Mecca. In the Christian world, the early veneration of martyrs led to the building of shrines (martyria) to house the relics or to commemorate the site of the martyr's suffering, to which the faithful would travel on the anniversary of the martyr's death.

Of all the sites for pilgrimage, those connected with the birth, ministry and death of Christ were the most important. The pilgrimage of the Empress Helena, the mother of Constantine, to the Holy Land in AD 326/8, during which she founded the basilicas on the Mount of Olives and at Bethlehem (and during which, according to legend, she discovered the True Cross), inspired many others to follow. Later, when journeys to Palestine became too dangerous due to Muslim incursions, pilgrimages to Rome and the shrines of St Peter and St Paul became much more common (25). The early Christian Church, however, was not always in favour of such journeys. In AD 370 St Gregory of Nyssa vociferously criticised pilgrimages, declaring that the false confidence in redemption caused those undertaking the pilgrimage to become careless of sin. Later, in the mid-eighth century, St Boniface warned that English whores lay in wait at towns and cities along every major pilgrimage route.

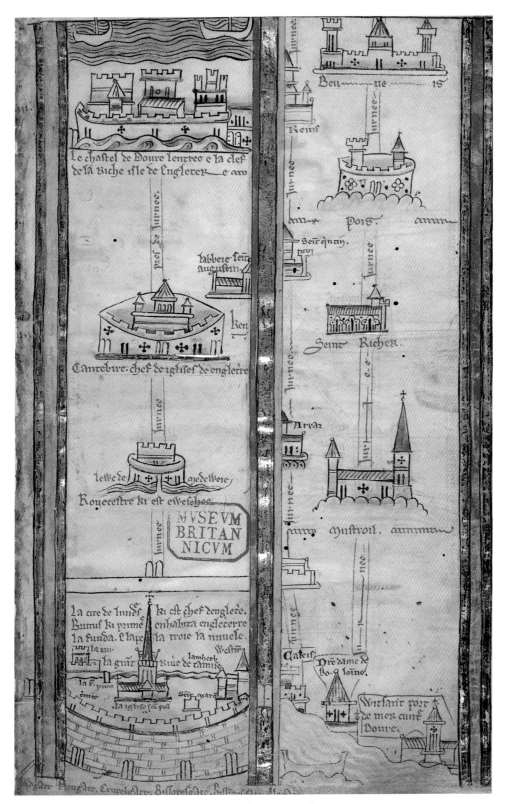

25. Pilgrimage route from London to Rome, 1250–59. Royal MS 14 C VII, f.2.

These concerns, by no means wild exaggerations, were not enough to ultimately dissuade the Church and as the concept of pilgrimage gained greater credence legal and ecclesiastical protection was granted to those undertaking such journeys. During the eighth century, the idea of a pilgrimage to a shrine being imposed as a specific part of a penance for a particularly grave sin was first introduced, and, by the ninth century, Jerusalem and Rome had been joined by many other locations as destinations for penitent pilgrims.

Pilgrimages inevitably imposed great strains on the towns and churches. A sermon given in AD 908 by Abbot Odo of Cluny, five years after St Martin at Tours – the church in which the sermon was delivered – was rebuilt, refers to the necessity of building churches with aisles as well as wide naves in order to prevent the great mass of pilgrims who periodically descended from overturning the choir stalls and

26. *Chaucer's pilgrims, c. 1455–62. Royal 18 D II, f.148.*

overrunning the choir. Pilgrimages could, however, bring rich benefits for the church concerned. Canterbury Cathedral acted with what might be regarded as unseemly haste to establish and spread the cult of Thomas Becket (d. 1170), with vials supposedly containing the martyr's blood being made available for pilgrims to purchase. The Pilgrims' Way rapidly became established, stretching across the southern counties of England from Winchester (the shrine of St Swithin) through to Canterbury (the shrine of St Thomas Becket). Chaucer's pilgrims (26), none too penitent if we judge them by the tales they tell on route, are following part of this path in *The Canterbury Tales*.

Excluding Rome, probably the most famous pilgrimage of the Middle Ages was to Santiago de Compostela in Galicia, north-west Spain. Pilgrims undertaking this journey would have gathered at towns and churches along the route – each one an important shrine in its own right – so by the time they reached their destination they would already have visited many sites of religious significance. This idea was not without a certain practical value – many of the routes to Santiago de

Compostela were infested with bandits so, consequently, there was an obvious appeal in travelling as part of a large group. Santiago de Compostela is the supposed resting place of St James the Great – the first apostle to be martyred, *c.* AD 44, by Herod Agrippa who had him beheaded. His body was 'discovered' in Spain in the early ninth century and taken to what is now Santiago (i.e. St James) de Compostela. Up until the thirteenth century St James was usually portrayed as a bearded individual carrying a scroll or a book but, in later depictions, he was distinguished from the other apostles by the attribute of a large floppy hat and a scallop shell (27). The scallop shell acted as a badge to show that the pilgrim had been to Compostela.

27. *St James the Great, with scallop-shells, late fourteenth century. Additional MS 23145, f.34v.*

SAINTS OF THE BRITISH ISLES

Many saints have a particular relevance to the people of the British Isles. Even the non-religious inhabitants of the countries they represent regard the four patron saints – George, Patrick, Andrew and David – with particular affection. To consider the saints of England, Ireland, Scotland and Wales as a whole is to consider the history of Christianity in these islands and to gain an insight into the various paths to sainthood. In Britain St Alban was venerated as far back as AD 429, and St Patrick (28) has been venerated in Ireland from the fifth century. St Alban was beheaded and, according to legend, at the

28. *St Patrick asleep, second half of thirteenth century. Royal MS 20 D VI, f.231v.*

29. *The martyrdom of St Alban, and the unfortunate consequences for his executioner, c.1250–60. Royal MS 2 B VI, f.10v.*

moment the sword struck the holy martyr's neck his executioner's eyes fell out – a detail that has been rendered with obvious delight by numerous manuscript illuminators down the ages (29). The early foreign Christian missionaries, such as Augustine and his followers from Rome, Aidan from Iona and Felix from Burgundy, were all canonized but it is only from the late seventh century that we began to have much detailed knowledge of English saints. Bede, important for biography as well as for history, records the lives of Saints Cuthbert, Benedict Biscop and Ceolfrith in addition to detailing the actions and achievements of many other English saints in his *Ecclesiastical History*.

Of the early English saints, Cuthbert (c. 634–687) (30) is perhaps the best known. Noted for the zeal of his preaching and teaching, he will forever be associated with Lindisfarne (Holy Island) in the north-east of England, where he spent much of his life. First prior and then bishop of the island, Cuthbert was buried on Lindisfarne in 687. Eleven years later, when the body was elevated to a shrine in the church, it was found to be incorrupt (31) – a sure sign of sainthood. When Vikings raided the island in 875, members of the community took the shrine

30. Cuthbert teaching at Lindisfarne, late twelfth century. Yates Thompson 26, f. 35v.

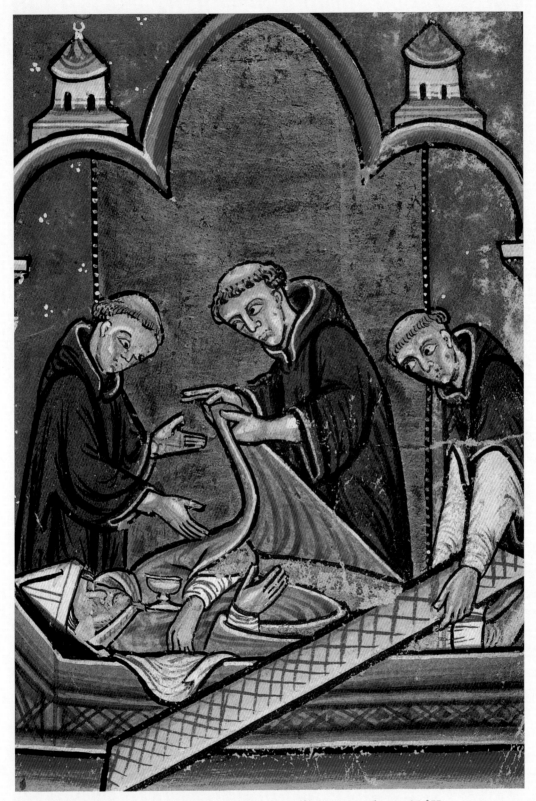

31. St Cuthbert's body is found to be incorrupt after eleven years, late twelfth century. Yates Thompson 26, f.77.

32. *An eagle catches a fish for St Cuthbert, late twelfth century. Yates Thompson 26, f.28v.*

and the saint's earthly remains and travelled around northern England and south-west Scotland with them, seeking a safe place for their reinterment. Finally they chose a permanent home in Durham in 995. A Saxon church was built over the shrine and Cuthbert's relics were translated into it in 999. When, in 1104, Cuthbert's relics were translated once more – this time to the new Norman cathedral in Durham – the remains were again found to be incorrupt. Towards the latter half of the twelfth century, a highly illuminated account of St Cuthbert's life was produced. The volume, which formerly belonged to Durham Cathedral, was at one time lent to Richard le Scrope, Archbishop of York (1398–1405) to provide models for a stained glass window in the Minster. The manuscript also supplied designs for paintings on the choir stalls of Carlisle Cathedral. Given the saint's love of birds (32) and animals, it is fitting that the Farne Islands are now a sanctuary for birds, seals and other wildlife.

Guthlac (AD 675–714) arrived at sainthood in a similar manner to St Cuthbert, although his beginnings were rather different. Born of royal blood, Guthlac was a Mercian nobleman who spent his early years raiding and looting the dwellings of the indigenous Britons. Later, in a considerable change of heart brought about by careful consideration of the shameful ends that the ancient kings of his family had met, he joined the double monastery at Repton in Derbyshire. Two years later he became a hermit in the fens at Crowland in Lincolnshire. Guthlac's reputation for holiness was built upon the miracles he performed, his affinity and respect for wildlife and his high standing as a spiritual guide to the many people who consulted him. Guthlac, famously, was also tormented and attacked by demons (33). To Felix, his East Anglian biographer, Guthlac, by turning to God, had exchanged one life of heroism and conflict for another. In place of the life of a nobleman and warrior, he had chosen a life of humility and reflection in which the human enemies he had previously faced were replaced by even more terrible supernatural foes. In couching Guthlac's spiritual battle in such terms, Felix gave the Anglo-Saxon nobility the sort of saint they could respect and admire, a saint whose spiritual battles mirrored their own secular troubles.

Two later Anglo-Saxon kings, Edmund of East Anglia (AD 841–869) and Edward the Confessor (1003–1066), also achieved sainthood: Edmund through imitation of Christ and Edward through a mixture of piety and political expediency. Abbo of Fleury's 'Life of St Edmund' became a key text in the ideology of the crusades. Faced with a vastly

33. *St Guthlac, menaced by demons*, c. 1210. *Harley Roll Y 6, roundel 7.*

superior force of invading Vikings, Edmund was given the choice of either submitting to the marauders or dying in battle. He chose the latter, not because he expected to achieve a resounding victory, or because he was too proud or patriotic to submit to the will of the invaders, but because as a *christus domini*, an Anointed of the Lord, he could not bow down before a pagan. For a Christian king the only way to deal with invading pagans was to fight them. If the Christian king is defeated, as Edmund was, then he would immediately be awarded a place in Heaven. All the images of St Edmund shown here (34, 35 and 36) are taken from a verse life written and illustrated by a monk of Bury, John Lydgate, and presented to King Henry VI. The manuscript shows the building of the abbey at Bury St Edmunds and also the young king, Henry VI, kneeling at the shrine of the saint. Henry VI was himself put forward for sainthood by Henry VII who

34. *Henry VI of England at the shrine of St Edmund, after 1433. Harley MS 2278, f.4v.*

saw this as a way of enhancing his claim to the throne. However, as Henry VII's position as the king of England became progressively more secure, and as his funds became rather more stretched, the proposal was dropped. Thus Henry VI, never the most fortunate of English monarchs, was denied his chance to become a saint.

35. *A wolf guards St Edmund's head, after 1433. Harley MS 2278, f.64.*

36. *The building of Bury St Edmund's Abbey, after 1433. Harley MS 2278, f.115v.*

King Edward the Confessor's reputation for holiness began in his own lifetime. His openness with his subjects, his generosity to the poor and the ill, his supposedly unconsummated marriage to Edith, the daughter of Godwin, Earl of Wessex, and the way in which he helped strengthen the ties between the old English Church and the papacy all counted in his favour. He also played a decisive role in the founding of Westminster Abbey. In spite of all these good works and deeds, however, the real reason why successive kings of England, from King Stephen onwards, petitioned the papacy for Edward's formal canonization was political. Contemporary sources fail to agree, but a considerable body of evidence suggests that King Edward promised William of Normandy the kingdom of England, only changing his mind on his deathbed and nominating Harold as his heir. By having Edward canonized, the Norman and Angevin rulers of England believed the legitimacy to the throne would be beyond dispute. Eventually, in 1161, Edward was canonized. Ironically, he was a popular saint with both the conquering aristocracy and with the subjugated labourers in the field, popular with the former because William claimed to be his rightful heir and popular with the latter because he was the last king of the old English line (37).

Henry II may have helped elevate Edward the Confessor to sainthood via his petitions to Pope Alexander III, but his role in the elevation of Thomas Becket to sainthood was altogether more direct. Thomas Becket (born c. 1120, archbishop of Canterbury 1162–70) was the most famous Englishman of the Middle Ages. Chaucer's 'holy, blissful martyr' was hacked to pieces one cold December evening in Canterbury Cathedral by four quite probably drunk knights, and thus was a life which had been characterised by vanity, conflict, pride and failure transformed into the very stuff of pious legend. Becket and Henry II had formerly been close friends, but, with Becket's elevation to archbishop, the pair had a succession of violent disagreements over subjects ranging from clerical immunity from prosecution in secular courts to the coronation of Henry the Young King by the Archbishop of York. The latter was an act on King Henry's part that was in blatant contradiction to one of the most cherished rights of Canterbury. However, by this stage Henry had been pushed so far by the stubborn behaviour of Thomas that he probably felt he had no alternative. After eight years of almost continual feuding, Henry, in a fit of temper, allegedly uttered the words 'will nobody rid me of this turbulent priest?' Four knights took the king at his word and on 29 December Becket was butchered in the north transept of

37. *King Edward, resembling Christ at the last supper, fourteenth century. Cotton Vitellius A XIII, f.3.*

his cathedral. In this illustration from a Psalter (38), written and illuminated in England c. 1200, one of the murderers, Reginald Fitzurse, is distinguishable by his coat of arms on his shield, a bear rampant. With the possible exception of the execution of Charles I, the death of Thomas Becket is probably the most chronicled act of wilful murder in English history. Five accounts were written by people actually in the cathedral at the time, including one by John of Salisbury, who cowered behind the altar as the violent scene was played out. Within three years of his death, Becket had been canonized and his tomb had become a focus for pilgrimage and healing. Within ten years, over 700 miracles were recorded. The Church, quick to take advantage of the cult and to cash in on the well-documented miracles, produced vials of Canterbury Water – supposedly an inexhaustible supply of the martyr's diluted blood – which were eagerly bought up by devout pilgrims.

38. The murder of Thomas Becket, c.1200. Harley MS 5102, f.32.

In life Becket had proved one of the least successful archbishops in English history, but in death his arrogance, vanity and pride were forgiven. It can be argued that his dying words: 'For the name of Jesus and the protection of the church I am ready to embrace death' form an epitaph that stands as the definitive definition of martyrdom.

The obvious question, when faced with the holy lives and inspiring examples provided by English saints such as Cuthbert, Guthlac, Edmund, Edward and Becket, is how did a fourth-century martyr who probably never set foot in the country become the patron saint of England? The answer revolves around the martial nature of the Middle Ages: the crusaders'

39. *William Bruges, first Garter King of Arms, kneeling before St George, fifteenth century. Stowe MS 954, f.5v.*

40. *An early representation of St Andrew with the Saltire cross, 1265–70. Additional MS 50000, f.8v.*

fight to reclaim the Holy Land and the later struggles against the French in the Hundred Years War. George is mentioned in an eighth-century martyrology of Bede, but it is with the Crusades that the cult of St George becomes firmly established within England. At the siege of Antioch a vision of saints George and Demetrius preceded the defeat of the Saracens and the fall of the town. When King Edward III (1327–77) founded the Order of the Garter, it was placed under St George's patronage (39).

The story of St George and the dragon became immensely popular in England during the late fifteenth century with Caxton's publication of *The Golden Legend*. It tells of how a community, terrorised by a dragon which had eaten their flocks, chose unfortunate human victims by the drawing of lots. When the king's daughter was chosen, she dressed as a bride to meet her fate but was rescued by St George, who pierced the dragon's side and captured it. George told the community that if they believed in Jesus and agreed to be baptised he would rid them of the dragon. They agreed and he killed the dragon. For his courageous act George accepted no payment, but instead asked the king to maintain churches and help the poor. The story has a great deal of colourful charm as a straightforward tale, but it can also be viewed as an allegory with St George defending the Church (the virginal daughter) from the forces of corruption and evil (the fire-breathing dragon).

St George was martyred at the very beginning of the fourth century, but during the Middle Ages he came to be regarded by the people of Venice, Genoa, Portugal, Catalonia and the English as the supreme example of Christian chivalry.

Just as there is a question about how St George became the patron saint of England, a similar question arises in Scotland. Andrew (d. *c*. AD 60) (40), apostle and martyr, never set foot in Scotland but legend relates that his relics were taken from Patras, Greece, to Scotland in the eighth century. The story survives in many forms, some of which suggest angelic intervention, and provides the reason why St Andrew is the patron saint of Scotland. Incidentally, the Saltire cross, the distinctive X-shaped cross which appears on the national flag of Scotland, only becomes common in representations of the martyrdom of St Andrew in the fourteenth century. The Saltire cross does make appearances in scenes of St Andrew's martyrdom as far back as the tenth century, but these are rare and the conventional cross was much more common.

IMAGES OF SAINTS
IN THE MEDIEVAL WORLD

Religious life in the medieval era was an intensely visual experience. The village church in its quiet rural landscape, no less than the cathedral in its bustling city centre, would have been embellished and enriched with images of saints. Images painted onto altar pieces, sculpted from stone, woven into tapestries, carved from wood and stained into glass. Many, especially those central to the Biblical stories such as the Virgin Mary, the archangel St Michael, St John the Baptist, the evangelists and the apostles, were known throughout the Christian world and were consequently depicted with great regularity.

41. St Michael, trampling on Satan and weighing souls, early fifteenth century. Additional MS 29433, f.194v.

42. St Christopher. *A day's grace from death, late twelfth century. Royal MS 2 A XXII, f.220v.*

43. *St Geneviève with her candle, 1525. Additional MS 18854, f.150v.*

Others, less universal in their significance, were often to be found only in particular isolated locations. Of the universally familiar, the Virgin Mary – accorded a position of pre-eminence among all the saints by virtue of being the Mother of God – was, by the end of the fourteenth century, represented in virtually all churches, abbeys and cathedrals in the form of a Lady Chapel. These chapels, graced with a painting or statue of the Blessed Virgin which provided a focal point for devotion, were structures of exceptional beauty. St Michael and St Christopher were represented with similar frequency. St Michael (41) was commonly depicted above the chancel arch in full view of the congregation, weighing souls to separate the saved from the damned. St Christopher meanwhile looked out over the pews from the north wall opposite the porch. It was commonly believed that looking upon an image of St Christopher granted the viewer a day's protection from death, exactly the sort of superstitious belief that was to be so fiercely condemned by Church reformers during the Reformation (42).

From an early date, depictions of particular saints became comparatively standardised. Pope Gregory the Great (AD 590–604) had referred to images as 'the books of the laity', and this notion certainly still applied in the Middle Ages. Images provided a way by which the great number of people who had no opportunity to learn to read could understand and follow events from the Bible and episodes from the lives of the saints. In order to be understood by all it was necessary for these images to be relatively unchanging. Artists focused on one particularly notable element from a story, something that would instantly call to mind the rest of the tale and give the viewer an immediate verification of just who was being portrayed. Often the particular element focused upon was connected with the saint's martyrdom: St Laurence with the gridiron on which he was roasted, or St Sebastian and the hail of arrows used to kill him. On other occasions a colourful episode or emblem from the life of the saint was chosen – St Margaret for example, emerging unharmed from the inside of a dragon-shaped demon which had devoured her, or the candle held by St Geneviève (43) which the devil repeatedly tried and failed to extinguish.

Saints were also present during times of quiet personal devotion, their images painted or printed onto the pages of Books of Hours and their lives described in hagiographic volumes. While some of the images in this book are taken from Psalters (liturgical books for personal use, containing the Psalms),

Missals (volumes containing the text of the Mass) and Breviaries (volumes containing the Divine Office), the majority are taken from Books of Hours. More Books of Hours were commissioned and produced, first as manuscripts and then later in printed versions, between the mid-thirteenth and mid-sixteenth centuries than any other text, including the Bible. The Book of Hours is a prayer book containing, as its central component, the Little Office of the Blessed Virgin Mary, or the Hours of the Virgin – a sequence of short services in honour of the Mother of God that were to be recited at various times throughout the day. Marian devotion placed the Virgin Mary in the supremely important role of intercessor between man and God. It was assumed that the Virgin would hear mankind's prayers and take up his cries for aid and solace with her son, who surely could not deny his mother. Often lavishly illustrated, a Book of Hours typically contained a sequence of a dozen or so suffrages (sometimes referred to as memorials) – petitions for aid from God via the intervention of a particular saint. The suffrages usually followed a particular order: The Holy Trinity (who were not, of course, saints), the Blessed Virgin Mary, the Archangel Michael and St John the Baptist (44) (the latter two being given particular importance as a consequence of their roles as judge and intercessor respectively at the last judgement), the Apostles (45), the male martyrs, the confessors, and the female saints led by the virgin martyrs. The text of the prayers was frequently accompanied by illustrations showing the saints in question. Local saints were included with their more illustrious counterparts in the calendars of these manuscripts (although illustrations depicting local saints in the suffrages are relatively sparse) and their presence often provides a clue to the location in which a particular Book of Hours was written. Lavish manuscripts produced for wealthy patrons often included an illustration of the person for whom the volume was intended, pictured with a patron saint. For example, a page from the Bedford Hours (46), shows Anne of Burgundy kneeling before St Anne, mother of the Virgin. The manuscript was written and illuminated for John, Duke of Bedford, and his wife Anne, sister of Philip, Duke of Burgundy, probably on the occasion of their marriage in 1423.

In literature *The Golden Legend*, a popular compilation of the lives of the saints put together by Jacobus de Voragine, a thirteenth-century archbishop of Genoa, became a much-loved source of inspiration for the European educated classes of

44. Martyrdom of St John the Baptist, fifteenth century. *Additional MS 11865, f.86.*

45. St John, apostle and evangelist, on Patmos, late fifteenth century. *Additional MS 35216, f.13.*

the Middle Ages. Manuscript copies of the text are still relatively common, providing a telling indication of its popularity. In 1483, William Caxton translated and printed *The Golden Legend* in England and the volume was reissued in one form or another a total of seven times before the Reformation, while the most important English collection of pious legends and miracles, John Myrc's *Liber Festialis*, went through nineteen editions between 1483 and 1532.

46. *Duchess of Bedford at Prayer before St Anne, 1414–23. Additional MS 18850, f.257v.*

THE REFORMATION

The Reformation began as a religious movement that set out to reform the practices of the Church and root out the widespread abuses of ecclesiastical privilege. As the sixteenth century progressed, however, the aims and tenets of the Reformation spread. Beginning with the doctrine of 'Justification by faith alone', Luther's belief in the Bible as the sole rule of faith, which led in turn to the rejection of all ecclesiastical authority (most notably that of the pope), caused a huge split in the Church. The cult of the saints came under widespread attack as reformers such as Luther and Erasmus exposed abuses connected with them, including deception and fraud. By rejecting papal authority they also rejected canonization – after all, there is no scriptural authorisation for canonization in the Bible. Images of saints came to be regarded by many as false Gods, a trap by which the unwary came to worship the saint, rather than worshipping God with whom the saint was meant to intercede. The smashing of images became commonplace. Counter-claims were put forward by people such as Thomas More who, while condemning the cult of obviously spurious relics and bizarre petitions for aid, added that such abuses were not approved of by Church authorities, nor were they approved of by rational well-informed believers. However, the violence against the images of saints within churches and on the pages of illuminated manuscripts went on. Henry VIII of England, who used the Reformation as a convenient excuse for splitting with Rome in order to legitimise his marriage to Anne Boleyn while his first wife was still alive, ordered the systematic dismantling of saints' shrines (to the immense gain of the royal treasury). In 1548 images of saints were ordered to be removed from all churches. Thomas Becket, who had of course famously stood up for the Church in a dispute with an earlier king of England, was 'decanonized' and all mention of him was ordered to be erased from liturgical books.

The medieval world itself was coming to an end and, with it, the heyday of the saints was drawing to a close. While a great deal of religious art was lost during the Reformation a substantial amount did survive, especially within the pages of manuscripts which were relatively small and portable and thus could be taken and hidden away by the faithful. Consequently, there are many images of saints and a great deal of medieval art which can still be enjoyed in the twenty-first century.

47. *Saints Apollonia, Claire, Lucy, Margaret, Barbara and Catherine, fifteenth century. Additional MS 27697, f.100v.*

FURTHER READING

The two most useful reference books are David Hugh Farmer, *Oxford Dictionary of Saints* (Oxford University Press, 1997, rev. edition), and Donald Attwater (Editor), *Penguin Dictionary of Saints* (Penguin Books Ltd, 1995, rev. edition). A wealth of information about saints can also be found at the www.newadvent.org website. Also very useful, and with an excellent introduction, is Jacobus de Voragine, *The Golden Legend* – Selections (Penguin Classics, 1998), which gives a modern, readable translation of the lives of the saints as they would have been known to the people of the late medieval world. For an informative and beautifully illustrated guide to saints in art see Rosa Giorgi, *Saints in Art* (Getty Publications, 2003). For more information on Books of Hours in general see Janet Backhouse, *Books of Hours* (The British Library, 1988), and Roger S. Wieck, *Painted Prayers: The Book of Hours in Medieval and Renaissance Art* (George Braziller Inc., The Pierpont Morgan Library, 1997). For a detailed discussion of the effects of the Reformation on Europe see Diarmaid MacCulloch, *Reformation: Europe's House Divided 1490–1700* (Allen Lane, 2003). For the effects of the Reformation on an isolated English community see Eamon Duffy, *The Voices of Morebath: Reformation and Rebellion in an English Village* (Yale University Press, 2001).

LIST OF MANUSCRIPTS ILLUSTRATED

Additional MS 11865	Book of Hours, France (Tours), 15th century
Additional MS 15702	Book of Hours, Flanders, c. 1474
Additional MS 18850	Bedford Hours, France (Paris), c. 1423
Additional MS 18851	Breviary of Isabella of Castile, Flanders (Bruges), before 1497
Additional MS 18854	Book of Hours, written and ornamented for Francois de Dinteville, Bishop of Auxerre, 1525
Additional MS 19416	Book of Hours, Flanders, late 15th to early 16th century
Additional MS 20694	Book of Hours, France, late 15th century
Additional MS 23145	Book of Hours, France, late 14th century
Additional MS 27697	Saluces Hours, Savoy, mid-15th century
Additional MS 29433	Book of Hours, France (Paris), c. 1407
Additional MS 35216	Book of Hours, France, late 15th century
Additional MS 50000	Oscott Psalter, England (perhaps Oxford), c. 1265–1270
Additional MS 54782	Hours of William Lord Hastings, Flanders (probably Ghent), c. 1480
Additional MS 74236	The Sherborne Missal, England (probably the Benedictine Abbey of St Mary's, Sherborne, Dorset), c. 1399–1407
Arundel 83	De Lisle Psalter, Englad (London or Westminster), c. 1308 with later additions
Cotton Galba A XVIII	Athelstan Psalter, Winchester (New Minster), second quarter of the 10th century
Cotton Nero D I	Lives of the Offas, Matthew Paris, England, c. 1250
Cotton Vitellius A XIII	Miscellaneous Chronicles, Anglo-French, c. 1280–1300
Egerton 2019	Book of Hours, France, latter half of the 15th century
Egerton 2125	Prayerbook of Joanna of Ghistelles, S. Netherlands (Bruges), between 1516 and 1529
Harley MS 2278	John Lydgate: 'Life of St Edmund', Bury St Edmunds or London, after 1433
Harley MS 2915	Book of Hours, England, by a French artist, c. 1450
Harley MS 2974	Book of Hours, 15th century
Harley MS 5102	Psalter, England (East Midlands?), c. 1220
Harley Roll Y 6	Guthlac Roll, East Anglia, c. 1210
Lansdowne 451	Pontifical, England (London?), 1420–1430
Royal MS 2 A XXII	Westminster Psalter, England (possibly St Albans), c. 1200 with later mid-13th century additions
Royal MS 2 B VI	Psalter from the Abbey of St Albans, England, mid-13th century
Royal MS 6 E VI	Omne Bonum, England (London), 1360–1375
Royal MS 14 C VII f. 2	Matthew Paris: Itinerary from London to Jerusalem, England, mid-13th century
Royal MS 15 E IV	Jean de Wavrin: 'Chroniques d' Angleterre', Flanders (Bruges), 1470s
Royal MS 18 D II	Works of John Lydgate, England, c.1460 with later editions, Flanders, c. 1520
Royal MS 20 D VI	Legends of Saints, French translations from Latin originals, northern France, 13th century
Stowe MS 594	William Bruges' Garter Book, England, 1440–1450
Yates Thompson 3	Hours of Jean Dunois, France (Paris), between 1436–1450
Yates Thompson 26	The Life of St Cuthbert, England (probably Durham), c. 1200
Yates Thompson 29	Ghislieri Hours, Italy (Bologna), c. 1500

INDEX

THE AUTHOR

Greg Buzwell is a Manuscripts Loans Curator in the Department of Manuscripts at The British Library and has worked on several large-scale exhibitions of medieval manuscripts.

Front Cover Illustration: *Detail of St Catherine of Alexandria trampling on a tyrant, c.1480. Additional MS 54782, f.68v.*

Half-title Page: *St James the Great, with scallop-shells, late fourteenth century. Additional MS 23145, f.34v.*

Frontispiece: *Christ enthroned with martyrs, confessors and virgins, ninth century. Cotton Galba A XVIII, f.21.*

Title Page: *Detail of God from an illustration depicting saints acting as mediators between the earthly and the heavenly, 1330–50. Royal MS 6 E VI, f.16.*

Back Cover: *St Christopher. A day's grace from death, late twelfth century. Royal MS 2 A XXII, f.220v.*

First published 2005 by
The British Library
96 Euston Road
London NW1 2DB

Text © 2005 Greg Buzwell
Illustrations © 2005 The British Library Board

British Library Cataloguing-in-Publication Data
A catalogue record for this book is available from The British Library

ISBN 0 7123 4870 0

Designed and typeset by Crayon Design, Brighton
Printed in Hong Kong by South Sea International Press